BILL CLINTON

BILL CLINTON

By Victoria Sherrow

DILLON PRESS
New York

Maxwell Macmillan Canada
Toronto

Maxwell Macmillan International
New York   Oxford   Singapore   Sydney

Photo Credits

All photos courtesy of AP—Wide World Photos

Book design by Carol Matsuyama

ISBN 0-87518-620-3
Library of Congress Card Number 93-1747

Dillon Press
Macmillan Publishing Company
866 Third Avenue
New York, NY 10022

Maxwell Macmillan Canada, Inc.
1200 Eglinton Avenue East
Suite 200
Don Mills, Ontario M3C 3N1

Macmillan Publishing Company is part of the Maxwell Communication Group of Companies.

First edition

Printed in the United States of America

10 9 8 7 6 5 4 3 2 1

CONTENTS

INTRODUCTION

A CROWD OF nearly 250,000 people stood waiting in the winter sunshine around the Capitol Building in Washington, D.C. It was January 20, 1993, and Bill Clinton was about to become the 42nd president of the United States. For decades, a traditional inauguration ceremony has marked the start of a president's four-year term in office. Citizens from all over America come to see the new president and witness this orderly change in the nation's leaders.

On this day, there was an even stronger spirit of change in the air. Bill Clinton was the first Democrat to be elected in 16 years, and he was the first Arkansan ever to hold the office. He was also the first president born after World War II (1939–1945), part of what is called the "baby boom" generation—people born between 1945 and 1962. At age 46, he was the second-youngest president in U.S. history.

Change had been a major theme during the 1992 election campaign, too. The candidates had talked about ways to improve the nation's economy, education, and health care. Bill Clinton had pledged to work toward needed changes in order to "make things work, to help people live up to their capacity . . . to solve problems [and] lift people up."

While Al Gore looks on, Bill Clinton takes the oath of office during the inaugural ceremony on Capitol Hill.

BILL CLINTON

Now Clinton placed his left hand on the family Bible held by his wife, Hillary Rodham Clinton. He raised his right hand and began to recite the oath of office: "I, William Jefferson Blythe Clinton, do solemnly swear that I will faithfully execute the office of president of the United States...."

It was a moment Bill Clinton had worked for and dreamed of for years. But when he was born in 1946, few people would have predicted he'd ever be president. His ancestors were poor Arkansas farmers. Nobody in his family had been famous; none had held public office. His father had died three months before his birth, and his widowed mother faced many problems raising a new baby alone.

Yet although they had little money, Bill and his mother, Virginia, were rich in other ways. They had a close, loving family with strong values. Virginia faced life with optimism and energy. Bill Clinton's early life taught him to be strong and to care about others. He learned that by setting goals and working hard, people could hope to reach their dreams.

His mother later said she had not had a specific dream about what Bill would do later in life. She had just wanted him to always do his best. Growing up, Bill Clinton showed that he was capable of outstanding achievement, both in school and later as governor of Arkansas. As president, he faced the greatest challenges ever in his 14 years in public office. There

Bill Clinton hugs his mother while his stepfather, Richard Kelley, looks on.

Clinton listens as an aide briefs him on the day's events.

were pressing problems at home in America and throughout the world.

In his inaugural address, President Clinton described these challenges. He pointed out that America and the world shared common concerns: "The world economy, environment, the world AIDS crisis, the world arms race—they affect us all." He talked about the need to help those who lacked jobs, housing, education, and health care, as well as the millions of poor children in the nation. He asked Americans to help themselves and each other.

The president also expressed his faith that by working together, people could make the world a better place. He said, "Americans have ever been a restless, questing, hopeful people. We must bring to our task today the vision and will of those who came before us. . . . Let us begin with energy and hope, with faith and discipline, and let us work until our work is done."

After a day of speeches and celebrations, President Clinton got to work. The new president rose early to begin his energetic first day in the White House. In 1963, when he was 16, Bill Clinton had shook hands with President John F. Kennedy in the Rose Garden outside this grand house. He had begun to dream of this job, with its heavy burdens and unique opportunities to improve people's lives. This time, Bill Clinton had come not as a visitor but to hold what many people call "the most powerful office in the world."

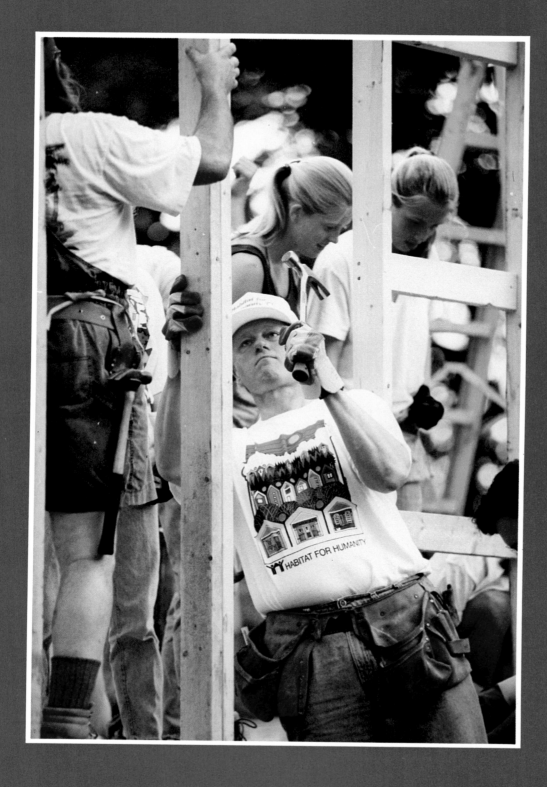

1
HARD WORK AND HIGH HOPES

THERE IS AN old saying about small towns in America: "People know when you are born and they care when you die." It was in that sort of place—the town of Hope, Arkansas—that Bill Clinton was born on August 19, 1946. Set amid woods filled with pine trees, the town has about 10,000 citizens. Many of them work in sawmills, small businesses, or on farms. Huge watermelons are grown in Hope, and it is known as the Watermelon Capital of the United States.

Bill Clinton's family had lived in Arkansas for four generations. Some of his ancestors were farmers in the Red River Valley. His mother, Virginia Cassidy, grew up in Hope, where her father, Eldridge, worked as a night watchman at a sawmill. Her mother, Edith, was a registered nurse. Virginia remembers her mother having great energy and ambition, qualities she and her son became known for, too.

While growing up, Virginia decided to study nursing, like her mother. She met Bill's father, William Jefferson Blythe III, in 1941. Blythe had brought a sick friend to the Shreveport, Louisiana, hospital where 18-year-old Virginia was a student nurse. They fell in love and were married. Soon Blythe left to serve in the army. America had entered World War II after

Bill helps frame a house at a Habitat for Humanity project in Georgia.

Japan bombed the U.S. naval base at Pearl Harbor, Hawaii, on December 7, 1941.

When the war ended in 1945, William Blythe came home. He and Virginia took up their lives together and were soon expecting a baby. Blythe sold auto parts and was planning to open a business in Chicago. One night, just three months before Bill was born, he died. He was driving home in heavy rain when a tire blew out and his car skidded off a slick road in Missouri.

Virginia named her new son William Jefferson Blythe IV after his father. Later, his mother would tell Bill that the father he had never met was a tall, handsome man known for his kindness. Virginia and her baby, called Billy, lived with her parents for two years after his birth.

When Billy was two, Virginia decided she needed more education in order to support them. She went to New Orleans in 1948 to become an anesthetist (someone who gives people medicine to make them sleep or so that they don't feel any pain when they have surgery). Billy stayed behind in Hope with his grandparents. Virginia later said that she'd wanted to give her son "the best possible chance," even though "it was terrible to leave him." Train tickets home were expensive, but the Cassidys were able to drive Billy to see Virginia twice while she was in New Orleans.

Early pictures of Billy show a pink-cheeked, bright-eyed boy. He was a quick learner who could read from the newspaper at age three, impressing his grandparents' friends. Billy enjoyed visiting the sawmill with his grandfather. There were large piles of sawdust where a little boy could play.

In 1950 Virginia completed her training and came back to Hope. Billy was then four years old. That year his mother married Roger Clinton, who owned a car business. Roger Clinton worked hard, and Virginia said he was a "loving parent." But it turned out that he had a drinking problem. Roger could become hot-tempered and unreasonable when he drank too much alcohol. Their home life was often tense and unpredictable.

As Billy grew up, he saw his stepfather out of control a number of times. Once Roger shot a gun in a room where Billy and his mother were standing. The bullet made a hole in the wall. Roger Clinton was taken to jail but later came back home.

Both Virginia and Roger worked all day, so Billy still spent many hours with his grandparents. The Cassidys had bought a grocery store, and Billy stayed there with them while they worked. His grandparents taught him to respect all people, regardless of their background or color. Their store and ice-delivery business served everyone. That was unusual in Arkansas in those days. Like other southern states, Arkansas

Bill learned compassion from his mother, who is accepting an award from the NAACP for her support of the civil rights movement.

had segregation laws that kept black and white people apart in restaurants, schools, churches, and other public places.

Bill Clinton has called his grandfather "the kindest person I ever knew." Besides teaching Bill to get along with others, Eldridge Cassidy talked to him about history and politics. He was a lifelong Democrat who had voted for Franklin Delano Roosevelt and Harry S Truman. Roosevelt had been president during the grim days of the Great Depression and World War II. Eldridge Cassidy praised FDR as a great and compassionate leader.

In 1953, when Billy was in second grade, his mother and

stepfather moved to Hot Springs, about 80 miles north of Hope. Hot Springs National Park, in the Ouachita Mountains, was a famous resort town. Steamy, mineral-rich spring water bubbled up from deep inside the ground there, and it was thought to have healing properties. Visitors came to use it in special baths.

The Hot Springs schools were larger than those Billy had attended in Hope. His mother sent him to St. John's Catholic School, which had smaller classes. During his two years there, the nuns at St. John's noticed how bright and studious young Billy was.

People who knew Bill Clinton recall that he also showed leadership qualities at a young age. His mother said, "He was always there when his playmates squabbled, and in minutes, he'd have both sides agreeing and playing together again." Sometimes when family members argued, Bill tried to settle things at home. He wanted people to talk out problems and resolve them without violence. His mother called him the "peacemaker" in the family.

Bill left St. John's to attend public school, first at Ramble Elementary. He continued getting good grades and was popular with his classmates. Outside of school, he liked reading, tag football, and basketball. Life at home stayed much the same. Virginia Clinton tried to keep the family together, despite

Roger's alcoholism. At times Roger was a fine husband and stepfather, good-humored and loving. There were happy days together, including picnics, church suppers, and holiday gatherings. But Bill and Virginia dreaded those times when Roger had his angry outbursts.

It was natural that Bill would sometimes wonder about the father who had died. As an adult, he said, "I imagined what it would be like to just see him come around the corner at Christmastime . . . what it would be like just to know what he had been."

In 1956 the family celebrated the arrival of a new son, named Roger Clinton, Jr. Bill was 10 years old and excited about being a big brother. Another thing that fascinated him that year was the 1956 presidential election. The Clintons now owned a television set, so Bill could watch the national conventions held by the Democratic and Republican parties. He listened to the candidates' speeches and began to understand more about government.

The next presidential election took place four years later, when Bill was in ninth grade. Massachusetts Senator John F. Kennedy, a Democrat, ran against the Republican vice president, Richard M. Nixon. Again, Bill watched with interest. His civics teacher at Central Junior High School told his students to listen to the debates and speeches so they

Roger Clinton, Jr., Bill's half-brother

could discuss the candidates' qualifications in class.

Bill was inspired by Kennedy and the speeches he made. In his inaugural address, Kennedy said, "Ask not what your country can do for you; ask what you can do for your country." President Kennedy's vision of a better world led many Americans to devote themselves to public service during the 1960s. Through the Peace Corps, some Americans went to live in other countries where they taught people useful skills. Others worked in American communities where people suffered from poverty, racial discrimination, and other problems.

Through the Boy Scouts and his youth group at the Park

Place Baptist Church, teenage Bill Clinton did community-service work, too. He raised money for charities. He knew many Arkansans lived in poverty. When he found out that Arkansas ranked lowest of all states in scores on school achievement tests, he told his mother he wanted to do something to improve that situation someday.

Virginia was proud of Bill's achievements. In talks with her sons and through example, she tried to stress the values of love, humility, integrity, and honesty. She often reminded the boys to "look a person straight in the eye when you talk to them." Bill Clinton would later be admired for his communication skills and the way he listened thoughtfully to people's concerns.

By the age of 15, Bill had grown taller than his stepfather. One night his parents were arguing, and Bill became so upset that he decided to confront his stepfather. He broke the locked door of their bedroom and told Roger, "Don't ever lay your hand on my mother again."

Virginia Clinton divorced her husband in 1962. She and the boys moved to another house, away from the ugly arguments. But a few months later, the couple remarried. Virginia had strong feelings about family ties and believed Roger when he promised to change. Bill was worried about the prospect of living with Roger Clinton again, but he was determined to help make things work. He had begun using the name "Bill Clinton," so his whole family would have the same last name. Now he made the change a legal one.

Despite problems at home, Bill still earned top grades in school and was known for his cheerfulness. Difficult times had made him more mature than most teenagers. Sometimes Virginia worked evenings at the hospital, and a woman named Earline White helped with the household chores. Mrs. White said, "Bill was obedient and didn't have foolish, childish ways." He was a big fan of the deep-fried apple and peach pies she baked for him and Roger. Another favorite dish was his mother's sweet-potato pie.

Besides Mrs. White, Bill knew few black people well. Hot Springs High School was all-white. But he valued the ideas of racial harmony he had heard at an early age. Bill was so moved by Martin Luther King, Jr.'s, 1963 "I Have a Dream" speech that he memorized it. With his friends, he sang folk songs that called for peace and racial harmony. In lighter moments, he entertained friends by imitating rock-and-roll singer Elvis Presley.

Bill also enjoyed jazz and began to play the saxophone. Talent and practice led him to be named school drum major, first saxophone in the band, and an all-state saxophone player. In addition, he was in the Beta Club, National Honor Society,

Bill Clinton as a teenager with his saxophone

chorus, Hot Springs Key Club, and Order of DeMolay, most
often as an officer. Because he was elected so often, the high
school passed a rule limiting how many offices one student
could hold at one time.

It seemed clear that Bill Clinton had a bright future.
Friends said the only question they ever had about his
grades was "whether he would make a high *A* or a low *A*." An

ex-classmate said Bill would "greet newcomers at school by saying, 'Hi, how are you? My name's Bill Clinton and I'm running for . . .' something, whatever it was. We always thought, well, someday, Bill will be president." An assistant principal also predicted, "He'll be president someday."

Paul Root, his tenth-grade history teacher, said Bill loved learning for its own sake, not just to get good grades. Bill and his friends discussed current events around the world. Bill later said how much he appreciated the encouragement his teachers gave him and the way they stimulated his thinking.

One of Bill's summer jobs was at a government-run camp. His mother said, "Every week he got a paycheck for $17." Yet Bill told his mother he felt guilty taking the money because he wasn't given much work to do. One week he came home without his pay. He told his mother he had mailed it to Washington, D.C., with a note saying he had not earned it. Surprised, Virginia realized just how seriously her son had taken lessons about honesty through the years.

During those early years, Bill Clinton tried hard to do well in each area of his life. Hard work had brought him good grades and the affection and respect of his family, teachers, and friends. Near the end of high school, Bill's efforts resulted in exciting opportunities, including a trip to meet one of his heroes.

2
NEW HORIZONS

IN 1963, WHEN he was a junior in high school, Bill Clinton was chosen as a delegate to Arkansas Boys' State. Boys' State and Girls' State are sponsored by the American Legion and held every summer in each state capital. During the week of activities, young people learn about government and meet political leaders. They run for various offices and set up a mock state government.

At Camp Robinson in Little Rock, Bill Clinton was elected a Boys' State senator. In July he represented Arkansas at Boys' Nation in Washington, D.C. It was thrilling, especially for a boy who'd had few chances to travel. Bill spent time in the Senate dining room talking with Arkansas Senator William Fulbright, the head of the Foreign Relations Committee. Then he found himself first in a line of young men who stood waiting in the Rose Garden outside the White House to meet President Kennedy.

A now-famous photograph of that memorable day shows Bill Clinton looking happy and respectful as he shakes hands with the president. His mother recalled that Bill seemed to have a new sense of purpose when he came home from the trip. Seeing his enthusiasm, she felt sure

Thirty years after his visit to the White House as a Boys' State delegate, Bill Clinton returned as the president of the United States.

he was going to pursue a political career.

Bill Clinton began his last year of high school excited about the future. His college plans were set. Impressed by his musical ability, Louisiana State University had offered him a music scholarship. But Bill had decided to attend Georgetown University, in Washington, D.C. He wanted to be part of that school's outstanding program for the study of international affairs.

On November 22, 1963, people around the world heard shocking news: President Kennedy had been shot and killed while riding in a motorcade in Dallas, Texas. Bill grieved that the dynamic, smiling man he had met that summer was gone. President Kennedy had stood for energetic leadership at home and abroad. His assassination seemed to begin a distressing time for America. A number of stormy and violent events were to cloud the rest of the 1960s.

Bill gradually adjusted to the loss of one of his heroes. In 1964 he graduated from high school with the fourth-highest grades in a group of more than 300 students. That fall he entered the Georgetown University School of Foreign Affairs.

Bill studied hard and made friends quickly at Georgetown. One close friend was Christopher (Kit) Ashby, from Texas. Ashby later recalled that other students said he and Bill had a southern accent: "But we didn't know it. We thought everyone else had an accent." Describing Bill, Ashby said, "He was intelligent and sharp. He was fun and had a great sense of humor. And he was very people-oriented."

Clinton balanced a heavy load of part-time work with classes in history, government, economics, and ethics (ideas about values and moral behavior). Friends liked to study with him because he was good at analyzing the material they had to learn in each subject. Bill Clinton served as class president for two years and took part in many activities, as he had in high school. He continued to read many books. One of his favorites was James Agee's *Let Us Now Praise Famous Men*, a novel about poor southern farmers.

Even with his scholarships and loans, Bill needed to work in order to pay for books, food, rent, and clothing. In his senior year, he got a job in Senator William Fulbright's office. He worked 20 hours each week for $55.

Bill admired Fulbright, who was respected for his fine mind and skills as a lawmaker. Fulbright had also begun to speak out against the Vietnam War in Southeast Asia. This meant that Fulbright had to oppose President Lyndon Johnson, his old friend and a fellow Democrat. Under Johnson's presidency, the war had expanded. Many Americans were fighting there, and thousands had already died.

In October of 1967, some Georgetown students took part

in a large antiwar march in Washington. Clinton did not join them, but his feelings against the war had become stronger. Each day in Fulbright's office, Clinton got to read the latest National Security Agency list of Arkansans who had died in Vietnam. Arkansas is a small state where many people know one another or have met each other's families or friends. Clinton often recognized the names on the list.

He was also dealing with a new personal crisis. His stepfather, Roger Clinton, had cancer. Knowing that Roger was dying, Bill visited home to help take care of him. When Roger was hospitalized in North Carolina, Bill drove to see him each weekend in the spring of 1967. The two men settled their differences before Roger died in 1968, when Bill was a senior at Georgetown.

Bill Clinton graduated during one of the most turbulent periods in U.S. history. In March, President Johnson said he did not plan to run for re-election. He wished to spend his last months in office trying to end the Vietnam War. Two of Johnson's fellow Democrats, Senator Robert Kennedy (John Kennedy's younger brother) and Senator Eugene McCarthy of Minnesota, were already campaigning against him as antiwar candidates. After Johnson's announcement, his vice president, Hubert Humphrey, also became a candidate.

In April, Martin Luther King, Jr., was assassinated in

A longtime supporter of civil rights, Bill Clinton talks with African National Congress leader Nelson Mandela and New York City mayor David Dinkins about the situation in South Africa.

Memphis, Tennessee. There were emotional riots in cities across America, including Washington, D.C. From Georgetown, students could watch the smoke rising from black inner-city neighborhoods. Friends recall that Bill Clinton was distraught. They heard him quietly repeating parts of King's "I Have a Dream" speech.

Clinton's friend and neighbor from Hot Springs, Carolyn Staley, had just come for a visit. Bill asked her to come with him to a relief center run by the Red Cross. He put a Red Cross sign on his white Buick. Then he and Carolyn drove food, medicine, and other supplies to churches in the burning neighborhoods.

In June another murder stunned the nation. Robert F. Kennedy was shot and killed in Los Angeles on the day he won the California primary election. Again, Americans mourned while they denounced the senseless violence. More riots plagued U.S. cities. The war in Vietnam continued, as more American bombs fell on Southeast Asia. People around the world debated whether the United States had a right to help the South Vietnamese army fight North Vietnamese troops.

In the midst of these events, Bill Clinton graduated from college. His 1968 Georgetown yearbook noted some of his achievements: Alpha Phi Omega fraternity; Who's Who; Student Activities Committee Chairman. Bill had received an honor that gave him the chance to study abroad, free, for two years: He was named a Rhodes scholar. With other distinguished college graduates from America and England, he would attend the famous Oxford University near London, England. When he called his mother with the good news, Bill asked, "How do you think I'll look in Harris tweed?" a reference to the clothing traditionally worn by British students.

That fall Bill Clinton left a dock in New York City aboard the SS *United States* headed for England. At first some of the men on the ship thought Bill was so friendly and idealistic he might not be sincere. The ocean was choppy, and a number of passengers got seasick. Bill brought them chicken soup and crackers. He played his saxophone to entertain the group. People soon realized his friendliness was real. "He was concerned about you," remembered Doug Eakeley, a Yale graduate on the ship who became one of Clinton's friends. "He'd wear you down with talk and understanding."

At Oxford Bill Clinton had the luxury of studying without having to work at extra jobs. He learned more about government and other subjects. For fun, he played rugby, a popular sport in England that resembles football. Bill and his friends hitchhiked around England. He later said that being at Oxford was "incredible. I got to travel a lot. I got to spend a lot of personal time—learn things, go see things. I read about 300 books both years I was there." In letters to his mother, he often said how grateful he was.

Nonetheless, Bill and other American men at Oxford shared a common worry. As college graduates, they were eligible to be drafted by the U.S. military. They might have to go to Vietnam. At that time, men had to register with a local draft board when they turned 18. If they were not in college and could pass the medical exam, they had to join the army.

Bill and his friends at Georgetown and Oxford had spent hours discussing this dilemma. Many of them, including Bill,

Bill Clinton (left) accompanies Senator George McGovern (center) during a campaign stop in Arkansas.

opposed the war. They had moral objections, as well as the fear that they might be killed or badly wounded in Vietnam for a cause they did not believe in. Some men who refused to go to Vietnam had left the United States to live in Canada; others had gone to jail rather than register or be drafted.

In the spring of 1969, Clinton got a letter from his draft board ordering him to report for an army physical in England. It meant he would be drafted when the school term ended. He and his friends talked all that night about what he should do. To avoid going to Vietnam, he decided to try to get into the army program for students called ROTC (a reserve officer training program). With Senator Fulbright's help, he was allowed to join the ROTC if he went to the University of Arkansas Law School. It meant giving up his second year at Oxford and his plans to attend Yale Law School.

During those months, Clinton thought about those who had died in Vietnam. He wrote to a friend, saying he might join the military because he felt guilty. In the meantime, Richard Nixon had been elected president in 1968. He started a new draft system called a lottery. Each day of the year was randomly selected and numbered: September 14 was number 1, April 24 was number 2, and so on. A person's birthday then determined what his draft number would be. Persons with low-number days would be drafted first.

BILL CLINTON

Clinton decided to take a risk. He told his draft board to reclassify him 1-A (ready for induction), so he could be in the lottery. At the same time, he did not withdraw from the Arkansas ROTC program. He went back to Oxford and waited to see what would happen. During the December lottery, he got a very high number, 311. That gave him little chance of being drafted. He withdrew from the ROTC program, writing a letter about his antiwar feelings.

After that Bill Clinton could plan his life without fear of the draft. In the fall of 1970, he accepted a scholarship to study law at Yale University, in New Haven, Connecticut. Clinton shared a beach house on Long Island Sound with some other students. Despite his busy schedule of studying and working, he made time to work for a candidate who was running for the U.S. Senate. Like other students, he enjoyed parties, dances, and other social activities.

In his second year at Yale, Bill Clinton met the woman who would become his wife and political partner. Hillary Rodham was also a law student at Yale. Bill had noticed his attractive classmate and been impressed by her intelligence. Once he had wanted to speak to her but felt too shy.

A few days later, Bill was talking to a friend in the law library. He kept glancing at Hillary, who was studying at the other end of the room. Finally, Hillary closed her book and walked over to Bill. She said, "Look, if you're going to keep staring at me, and I'm going to keep staring back, I think we should at least know each other. I'm Hillary Rodham. What's your name?"

Bill Clinton later admitted that, at that moment, he had trouble remembering his name. As he got to know Hillary better, he found that they shared common interests and goals. At one point he said to himself, "This woman is 'trouble'—the one I could love." In the summer of 1972, they worked together in Texas to coordinate Senator George McGovern's campaign for president. They missed the start of school that fall in order to keep working on the campaign. Yet they awed their friends by getting top grades on all their exams.

When they graduated from law school in 1973, Bill and Hillary went in different directions. Hillary took a job in Washington, D.C., working for a committee of the House of Representatives. As for Bill Clinton, he had always known where he would go after graduation—not to Washington or to a big-city law firm in New York or Boston, but back to his roots: Arkansas.

3
MAKING A
DIFFERENCE

BEFORE HE WAS killed in 1968, Robert Kennedy used to say that, "One man can make a difference, and every man should try." Bill Clinton believed that with his education, ideas, and desire to improve life in Arkansas, he could make a difference. His first job after coming home in 1973 was teaching law at the University of Arkansas in Fayetteville.

Bill kept in touch with Hillary Rodham by phone. He invited her to visit his family. When she arrived, Bill picked her up at the airport and drove her around the area to see some of his favorite places and sample some Arkansas cooking. Hillary stayed with Bill's mother, Virginia, and her third husband, Jeff Dwire.

In 1974 Bill was delighted when Hillary decided to join him as a law professor at the university. She had turned down several high-paying jobs at law firms elsewhere to move to Arkansas. When Hillary arrived, she immediately began working on a new political campaign—this time, Bill's.

At the age of 28, Bill Clinton was running for the state congress. His campaign office was a two-room wooden shack near the university. He was running against a popular Republican congressman in a mostly Republican district. In his 1970

Clinton attends a meeting at the White House during the early days of his career as governor.

Gremlin, Clinton drove around the district to talk with voters.

Although he lost that election, Bill impressed many voters. He came close to winning, getting 48 percent of the vote to the winner's 52 percent. The Arkansas Education Association had supported his candidacy. An article in the Arkansas *Gazette* referred to Clinton as "a brilliant young law professor." It predicted that he would run again in the 1976 election.

In the meantime, Bill was sure that he wanted to marry Hillary Rodham. He decided to surprise her by buying a house she had admired during one of their drives together. One day he announced, "I've bought that house you like."

Hillary remembered the small house with the bay window beside a lake. But she pointed out, "I've never been inside it."

"Well, I thought you liked it, so I bought it. So I guess we'll have to get married now," he told her.

Their families helped the couple paint the rooms inside the house before they were married in October 1975. The wedding was a quiet one, attended by their families. More than a hundred guests came to the backyard reception that followed. Then Bill and Hillary flew to the resort city of Acapulco, Mexico, for their honeymoon.

The couple continued teaching law in Fayetteville while settling into married life. Friends joined them for long dinners at which they discussed their many interests: law, politics,

Clinton takes care of some business during his term as Arkansas attorney general.

music, art, books, and national and world news. That year saw one sad event: Bill's mother, Virginia, became a widow for the third time when her husband died of diabetes.

Bill was elected attorney general of Arkansas in 1976. That meant that he handled the legal affairs for the state. Part of his job was to watch public utilities—such as phone, gas, and electric services—to help keep prices fair. People in the state thought he worked hard. They liked the way he took time to

Bill and Hillary during his first term as governor

answer their calls and letters and talk about their problems.

In 1978 Clinton decided he was ready for the challenge of being governor. His opponents said that, at age 32, he was too young and inexperienced. But the voters elected him, making Bill Clinton the nation's youngest governor. Hillary, meanwhile, had become known as an outstanding lawyer. She worked at a prestigious law firm in Little Rock, where she and her husband lived in the governor's mansion.

From the start of his two years as governor, Bill hoped to improve Arkansas's schools. The schools were often criticized, and students' test scores had been the lowest among all 50 states. Some of the things Bill wanted to do, such as raising teacher's salaries, would cost extra money. Taxes in Arkansas were low, so he raised the fees people paid when they got new car or truck licenses. Some of this money would go to improve roads too.

Many people resented paying these higher license fees. Other changes Bill made as governor were also criticized. Some doctors disliked the rural health clinics he set up. Owners of large companies disliked paying higher taxes. Citizens resented the fact that he hired experts from other states to work in his administration, to solve local problems.

In early 1980, Bill Clinton became a father. He and Hillary were thrilled to welcome daughter Chelsea Victoria Clinton on February 27. While standing in the delivery room for the birth, Bill felt lucky. Unlike his own father, he had the opportunity to love and care for his child. He looked forward to being a devoted parent.

More problems arose for him as governor, however. During a hot, dry spring and summer, farm businesses lost many chickens and other livestock. Fires damaged two state forests. Clinton had not caused these problems, but they seemed to increase the feeling that things were not going well during his term of office. In the fall of 1980, he lost his race for re-election.

One person explained Clinton's loss by saying that people in the state seemed to think he "had gone off to get a fancy

As governor, Clinton tried to get to know the day-to-day problems of the people in his state, like this dairy farmer.

education and brought home a fancy wife and had gotten too big for his britches." During the campaign, his wife had been criticized for using her maiden name, Hillary Rodham, as a lawyer. Many women kept their former names during the 1970s and afterward. But many Arkansans preferred more traditional roles for women. They thought wives should follow the custom of using their husband's name.

Bill had worked hard, and he hated to leave office before

he could achieve his goals for the state. In January of 1981, he made a farewell speech to the Arkansas legislature. He said he hoped people would remember him "as one who reached for all he could for Arkansas."

The Clintons left the governor's mansion, but Bill did not give up his dream of leading the state. He thought about what had gone wrong while he was governor and what he could have done better. Soon he began to make speeches, in person and through television ads. He apologized to voters and said he had learned from his mistakes, such as making too many changes too fast.

Bill drew strength from his religion after he lost the 1980 election. He was a member of the Imanuel Baptist Temple in Little Rock, where he sang in the robed choir. Spiritual music was something he had loved for many years. Among his favorite hymns were "Eternal Life," "Holy Ground," and "Amazing Grace."

Hillary encouraged Bill and supported his effort to be elected again. She wanted to work with him for causes they cared about, such as education, health care, and children. Hillary had spent years helping children. Since college, she had worked with a group called the Children's Defense Fund. She devoted many hours, without pay, to helping poor children and those who suffered from abuse or neglect. To help Bill, Hillary began using his last name, since it seemed to mean a lot to people in Arkansas.

When Clinton was elected governor again in 1982, he had thought carefully about how to carry out his plans. He asked the state legislature to help him bring more jobs to Arkansas and to improve the schools. The lawmakers worked with him to pass stricter laws against drunk drivers.

Governor Clinton asked his wife to head the Arkansas Education Standards Committee. He believed Hillary could do an outstanding job leading the group. The committee members traveled throughout the state, meeting with school administrators, teachers, parents, and students. Hillary listened carefully. She helped the group examine the many problems that people discussed during these meetings.

The committee made several recommendations. It backed a law that required teachers to pass a basic skills test. Governor Clinton said if teachers did not pass the test, they "should be required to improve those basic skills if they're going to remain in the classroom." He approved higher salaries for teachers and better school facilities. Students were now required to take a test when they started high school so teachers could judge their progress. Clinton also urged parents to attend PTA (Parent–Teacher Association) meetings.

While leading the committee, Hillary became known as

an expert on education. She still worked at her law firm and served on several boards across the nation, including the Children's Defense Fund, Wal Mart Department Stores, and the Children's Television Workshop. In addition, she had many duties as First Lady of Arkansas. Hillary planned her schedule carefully so she could enjoy important family time with Chelsea and Bill.

In 1983 Bill Clinton faced a personal crisis. Police told him an undercover operation had shown that his half-brother, Roger, then 28, was selling illegal drugs. Bill knew that during the next month, Roger would be arrested along with others who were breaking the law. Roger was sentenced to a year and a half in jail. Upset, he said that he thought Bill had let him down.

When he left jail, Roger, Bill, his mother, and Hillary took part in family counseling discussions. They grew closer and learned to understand one another's needs and feelings better. Virginia also joined Al-Anon, a support group for family members of people who are addicted to alcohol or drugs. Roger worked hard to overcome his drug problem. He began a career as a musician and later became a production assistant for a TV show in Los Angeles.

Bill Clinton was re-elected governor in 1984 and again in 1986. He and Hillary continued working hard for education.

Clinton celebrates another victory as governor.

They expanded programs that helped preschoolers get ready for school. Another ongoing project was improving health care. Hillary led an effort to bring the first neonatal care units to Arkansas. Now newborn babies with special needs could get expert help in this hospital unit. A helicopter service called Angel One was started to bring emergency help to people in remote parts of the state.

Clinton's education programs were praised in other states, some of which developed similar teacher-testing programs. Student test scores were improving, and fewer high-school students were quitting before graduation. Slowly, the number of college-bound students was rising too. Arkansas led the states in its region in the number of new jobs.

National leaders and the heads of the Democratic party began to notice the dynamic Arkansas governor and his multitalented wife. They were pleased by Clinton's successes. With his youth, friendly ways, and energetic leadership ability, Bill Clinton seemed headed for larger roles on the national political scene.

4
A NATIONAL ROLE

DURING THE LATE 1980s, Bill Clinton took on some jobs that brought him national attention. In June 1986, he became cochairman of the National Governors Association task force on welfare reform. Then he was named chairman of the Governors Association. Accepting this job in August of 1986, Clinton told his fellow governors that their top priority should be creating more jobs. He said that the nation must "find ways for Americans to be able to work and have work."

Clinton began his fourth term as governor on January 13, 1987. He asked his fellow Arkansans to look ahead to what they could achieve by working together, regardless of political beliefs. To the state legislature, he said, "You can be proud of what you've done and what we've been able to do together." He asked them to continue improving education so that young people would be prepared for the challenging new jobs they would face in the future.

By now Clinton was being recognized as a leader in the growing effort to improve America's schools and its work force. He went to Washington, D.C., several times to discuss these topics with President Reagan and various groups. In February of 1987, he gave a speech there that discussed ways in which

Bill Clinton chairs a meeting of the Governors Association.

schools could work together with businesses to create more jobs and train better-qualified workers.

People began to wonder if Bill Clinton might run for president in 1988. Reporters asked him if he would be a candidate. Bill had decided against it. He did not want to be away from home for so many months campaigning for the primary elections held in different states. Chelsea was only seven years old, and he felt they would miss each other a great deal during an important year in her life. He was also eager to complete his work in Arkansas, especially for education. He told reporters that the people had elected him to do a job and he meant to do it.

Massachusetts Governor Michael Dukakis became the party's choice for president that year. Clinton agreed to give the speech nominating him at the Democratic national convention. It turned into an embarrassing moment for Bill. He worked hard on his speech and rewrote it nine times. When he practiced the speech, it took about fifteen minutes, the amount of time allowed.

When Bill spoke at the convention, people cheered each time he said Dukakis's name. He wanted people to hear about Dukakis, so he kept talking—for more than 30 minutes. People voiced their impatience, and TV newspeople criticized him for talking so long. When he was done, Clinton bravely faced the critical reporters in the press room. The next day other people, including comedian Johnny Carson, made fun of the speech. To show that he was a good sport, Clinton appeared on Carson's show the next night. He joked about the incident and played his saxophone with the NBC orchestra.

Bill said that his friends in Arkansas were understanding during this time of negative publicity. Anyway, he had survived much tougher times in his life. He had learned to face setbacks and go on. It was a philosophy of life Clinton saw in his mother, who once said, "Life *is* tough. That's what builds character: being able to take life's blows and not whine about it."

In 1988 the people of Arkansas again elected Bill Clinton as their governor. He pledged to keep working for better education and job training that would let people learn all through their lives. At a news conference, Clinton introduced citizens who had benefited from these programs. One man had learned to read in adult education classes; a woman had left welfare for a good job after getting more training and a high-school diploma. Clinton said that America now had to compete with countries that "have better-educated work forces and are investing more money in people and economic development."

Governor Clinton was pleased when newly elected President George Bush said that education should be a national

BILL CLINTON

priority. The president called for an education summit—a special meeting to discuss problems and possible solutions. Bill joined the president, other governors, and education experts in Charlottesville, Virginia, in September of 1989. He led many of the discussions and took a major role in setting the six national goals for education.

At home Clinton continued his work and enjoyed spending time with his family. One of his morning routines was driving Chelsea to school. Bill and Hillary liked to watch Chelsea play softball and dance in ballet recitals. The Clintons also enjoyed playing cards and board games together. They went on bicycle rides and watched movies, sometimes while eating take-out pizza. Like many people, Bill Clinton admitted he enjoyed rich foods and sometimes craved doughnuts and other sweets. He tried to exercise every day, often jogging outdoors to keep fit and healthy.

In June of 1991, the nation's governors named Bill Clinton the most effective governor in America. That same year, Bill decided he would run for president in the upcoming 1992 election. It meant campaigning hard for the nomination, since several other Democrats were planning to run. If nominated, Bill would be up against a popular president, Republican George Bush. Even so, he believed that some things in America needed to change. He wanted

A young Chelsea accompanies her father as he votes during an election in Arkansas.

to lead the country through those changes.

A presidential campaign would also make demands on his family. Bill and Hillary talked it over. They were excited about working on education, jobs, and health care on a national level. As for Chelsea, she was 11 years old and in seventh grade that year. She was busy with schoolwork, friends, sports, and dance lessons. Happily, her grandparents, the Rodhams, had moved to Little Rock, and she saw them often. Chelsea did not object to the idea of her parents spending time away from home campaigning.

On October 3, Bill Clinton announced his candidacy at the Old State House in Little Rock. He said, "I refuse to stand by and let our children become part of the first generation to do worse than their parents. I don't want my child or your child to be part of a country that's coming apart instead of coming together." America could change for the better, he said, and still keep its values: "work, faith, family, individual responsibility, and community."

Discussing the nation's problems, Clinton stated, "Middle-class people are spending more hours on the job, spending less time with their children, bringing home a smaller paycheck.... Our streets are meaner, our families are broken, and our health care is the costliest in the world." As president, Bill Clinton promised to try to get Americans to work together "to give new life to the American dream."

It was the start of a tough campaign. Clinton was not well known outside of Arkansas. He visited many cities to meet voters and explain his ideas. Early on, he had to answer charges that he had tried to get out of being drafted by the army when he was a Rhodes scholar. Some people called his actions unpatriotic, while others supported his opposition to the Vietnam War. Bill Clinton defended his actions and told people about his achievements as governor. He and Hillary answered questions about their family life to show people they had a strong, happy marriage.

Over a period of months, Bill Clinton became the leading Democratic candidate. Finally, he had gained enough votes to be the Democratic nominee for president. The convention was held in New York City in July of 1992. Bill's acceptance speech stressed the same things he had worked for as governor: better education and health care and more opportunities for Americans to get jobs.

In his acceptance speech, Bill Clinton shared some personal feelings. Many people thought Bill Clinton was a rich politician whose parents had sent him to expensive schools. He wanted Americans to know where he had come from and what he stood for. So Bill told how his mother had worked hard to get more education and to keep her family together. Then he said, "My grandfather just had a grade-school education. But in that country store he taught me more about equality in the eyes of the Lord than all my professors at Georgetown; more about the intrinsic worth of every individual than all the philosophers at Oxford; and he taught me more about the need for equal justice than all the jurists at Yale Law School."

After the convention, people realized Bill Clinton had been through rough times and had worked hard for his education. They saw that he was friendly and cared about people. But he still had to defend himself against attacks by his opponents. He was accused of not knowing enough about foreign policy or how to run the economy. And he was still being criticized for his draft record.

Bill knew he must campaign hard to win. Besides George Bush, another major candidate named Ross Perot was running for president. Many people liked what Perot was saying, and he had a large personal fortune to spend on his campaign. Polls showed that the race among the three men was close. Clinton traveled all over America for debates, speeches, and other appearances. At times he became hoarse from speaking so often.

Hillary campaigned a great deal, too. The Clintons planned their schedules so that they could spend time together whenever possible. Bill spoke to Hillary and Chelsea by phone at least once a day. Sometimes he helped Chelsea do her algebra homework long-distance. He could not fly to Little Rock every three or four days as Hillary did, but he got home for Chelsea's dance recital and other important events.

Bill had picked Tennessee Senator Albert (Al) Gore as his vice-presidential running mate. Gore was a popular senator who knew much about foreign affairs and arms control. He had written a well-reviewed book on the environment. Clinton

Clinton and running mate Al Gore announce their partnership to a cheering crowd.

thought Al Gore was capable and intelligent. He believed they would make a fine team.

Al and his wife, Mary Elizabeth, called Tipper, often joined the Clintons on a campaign bus tour. The four became friends. They met and talked with people in small towns as well as large ones across the country. Sometimes Bill asked the bus driver to stop so they could meet people who were waiting beside the road to see the candidates. One farmer in Iowa waited more than an hour to see the campaign bus. After Bill had stopped to shake his hand, the farmer said that it was a good idea for the candidates to visit towns like this to talk with people. "Maybe they'll learn something," he commented.

BILL CLINTON

All the candidates appeared on morning talk shows, evening interview shows, and even MTV, the cable music-video station. Bill talked and played his saxophone one night on the "Arsenio Hall" show. He and the other candidates

A strong advocate of the power of young people, Bill Clinton answers questions from young Americans during an MTV special.

answered questions by viewers who called in to talk shows. As the election approached, the Clinton-Gore ticket was leading in the polls. More voters thought they offered practical ideas about problems like high health-care costs, unemployment, crime, and homelessness.

Despite his lead, Clinton did not slow down, even when he became hoarse, then lost his voice. Once Hillary had to finish a speech for him after his voice had failed. To reach more people, Clinton flew from city to city in the weeks before the election.

Bill Clinton amazed many people by his stamina during the campaign. There were times people had predicted he would give up. Bill was surprised by that outlook. He later said, "My mother and my family gave me this sense of resilience and just enjoying life. . . . Most of the family were living in quite modest circumstances, had grown up in the Depression or before. Never had much of anything. They had the idea that nobody owes you anything, you're not entitled to anything good, you gotta take what comes, and you just can't give up. Quitting is a form of cowardice, and you just can't do it."

That kind of attitude kept Bill Clinton going. In the two days before the election, he flew more than 5,000 miles to campaign in 14 different cities. His voice worn out, he returned to Little Rock to await the decision of the American people.

A smiling supporter holds up a copy of Clinton's hometown newspaper the morning after his presidential win.

5
MR. PRESIDENT

AMERICANS VOTED IN record numbers on November 3, 1992. Many people had decided that the outcome of this presidential election was very important. Voters had had more chances to see, hear, and talk with the candidates through television than ever before.

That evening, Bill Clinton's friends and supporters in Little Rock watched the election returns on a huge television screen tuned to the Cable News Network. A map of the United States showed how people across the country had voted that day. Each time a state voted for Clinton and Gore, it was filled in with the color blue. The group cheered as most of the states on the map became blue. They counted the number of votes, knowing that Clinton needed 270 of the possible 538 state electoral votes in order to win.

By winning the state of Ohio, Clinton went over that number. Despite a strong showing by Ross Perot (19 percent of the vote), Clinton had been elected president. He had received 43 percent of the votes, and George Bush had won 38 percent.

After the results had come in, Bill's mother told him, "I love you, and I'm so proud."

BILL CLINTON

Crowds of people were gathered at Little Rock's Old State House when President-elect Bill Clinton gave his victory speech around midnight. He and Al Gore and their families looked joyful and excited. Smiling, he thanked the people who had worked on his campaign and voted for him. He said that people had shown "high hopes and brave hearts" in choosing to make a change in the nation's leadership. Clinton asked all Americans to work with him. He said, "Together we can make the country we love everything it was meant to be." Bill and Hillary danced briefly to a song that had become a theme in the campaign: "Don't Stop," by the rock group Fleetwood Mac.

After the speeches, Bill went to the Camelot Hotel Ballroom next door for a victory party. The night before the election, he had not slept at all. Election night, he had about three hours of sleep. Even so, there was work to do the next day. After breakfast, Clinton began preparing to go to Washington. One big task was to choose qualified people to serve on his staff and cabinet. He must also prepare a budget to give Congress early in 1993. Clinton and President Bush met for briefings, at which they discussed national concerns and an orderly change in the government.

Besides that, Clinton wanted to fulfill his promises to the voters. During the 1992 campaign, he had listed these goals:

1. To improve educational opportunities for all.
2. To increase job opportunities for everyone who wants to work.
3. To protect our environment, especially the rain forests, the wetlands, and the Arctic Refuge.
4. To reduce crime with tough laws and better rehabilitation programs.
5. To reduce the drug problem with tough laws and drug prevention programs.
6. To help the homeless and the poor by providing jobs and education.
7. To make life better for all Americans—rich, poor, healthy, sick, young, old—so that we can *all* enjoy living in such a great country.

Clinton hoped to get off to a fast start and be able to offer some new plans and programs within his first 100 days in office. He said that the days after the election were keeping him even busier than he had been during the campaign.

Bill also had some final duties as governor. Preparing to go to Washington, he spoke of his desire to keep in touch with his roots in Arkansas: "The roots I have here mean a lot to me. It was an important reason I was elected. People read that I come from a real place. That I have real friends. That I had a real life. I must say that I am excited about the future, but I am going to miss this place terribly."

BILL CLINTON

During the week of the inauguration, Bill and Hillary left Arkansas for many public appearances and celebrations. Clinton had decided to take a bus tour along the route Thomas Jefferson followed when he became president in 1801. After attending church on January 17, the Clintons boarded a bus near Jefferson's home in Monticello, Virginia, and rode to Washington, D.C. That same day, there was an outdoor festival at the Mall in Washington where visitors could see American crafts while sampling foods from different regions and listening to American music. More than 200,000 people visited the 52 tents that lined the Mall.

The Clintons had said they wanted more people, including those who were not famous, to be able to attend some of the week's events, called "An American Reunion." They held an American Citizens' Lunch, a Salute to Youth at the Kennedy Center, and many other large celebrations.

Then came the day of the inauguration itself. Bill Clinton's 14-minute speech was shorter than those of many past presidents. Standing before the large crowd, many of them waving U.S. flags, Bill Clinton looked very moved. During his speech, he praised the outgoing president, George Bush, for his 50 years of service to America. He spoke of the work to be done in America and the need to work together to do it.

Clinton had asked one of his favorite poets, Maya Angelou,

Clinton joins Michael Jackson and Stevie Nicks of Fleetwood Mac onstage at an inaugural concert.

to write something for his inauguration. Her poem, "On the Pulse of Morning," echoed ideas that Clinton had stressed in his campaign: the rich diversity of America's people and the need for change so that America could reach its full promise. "Give birth again to the dream," said Angelou.

That day, Bill, Hillary, and Chelsea moved into 1600 Pennsylvania Avenue. President Clinton took up his new job with enthusiasm. He appointed the remaining members of his cabinet. He finished his budget. In February he delivered a speech to Congress.

Bill had often called his wife a person of "many talents" who would be a great partner in the White House. In February of 1993, he appointed Hillary Rodham Clinton to head the health-care reform group. Her work for education, children, and health care had made her well qualified. Among other things, she had helped to enlarge the Arkansas Children's Hospital, then set up programs to train doctors for poor children in rural areas. Hillary had been called a leader who could grasp difficult problems and find practical solutions.

During those first months in office, President Clinton seemed to love his job. Despite heavy responsibilities, Clinton looked cheerful and kept the positive attitude he had shown in the campaign. He worked long days writing speeches, studying facts and figures, attending meetings, and discussing plans with his staff.

One setback occurred when he found out that the U.S. economy had more problems than he thought. The nation had a larger debt than what Clinton had been told before the election. It would be harder to find money for new programs and still reduce the national debt. President Clinton called together experts on financial matters to

First cat Socks gets his first taste of meeting the press with a little lift from a photographer.

work with him on these problems.

The Clintons adjusted to their new home. They welcomed their cat, Socks, to the White House. A family friend drove him there from Arkansas. Bill Clinton started jogging each morning on a track built inside the White House grounds. Chelsea sometimes brought her homework to the presidential study next to the Oval Office where her father worked. The family

Bill and Hillary celebrate at one of the many inaugural balls held in their honor.

rooms looked homier as the Clintons arranged their favorite things, including a collection of books by Arkansas writers.

Bill and Hillary also began entertaining people. They had started the day after the inauguration with an open house for many visitors. At formal dinners, they featured American cooking with fine foods from around the country. At family meals, Bill sometimes requested chicken enchiladas. He liked vegetables and fruits, including his favorite, bananas.

Chelsea took friends on a White House scavenger hunt during a sleepover party. The family tried out the White House bowling alley and screened movies in the private theater.

President Clinton knew that people had put a lot of trust in him to lead the country in this last decade of the 20th century. He said, "The voters have so much hope now for us to do things. They want us to get out there and get things done and show some movement." Many programs, like education reforms, don't always show quick results. President Clinton said he wanted people to look beyond the present and toward the future. He thought that people could do that if he communicated well with them about his programs. Both Bill and Hillary said they thought the White House was the best place to achieve the things they cared about. President Clinton said, "I'm just going to do the very best I can and try to have a wonderful time doing it."

Index

About the Author

BEFORE BECOMING A full-time writer, Victoria Sherrow worked in the field of community mental health. She is the author of more than 30 books for young people, including *Cities at War: Amsterdam*, *Challenges in Education*, *Separation of Church and State*, and *Image and Substance: The Media in U.S. Elections*. Her other biographies include books about Phillis Wheatley, Jonas Salk, Mahatma Gandhi, and Hillary Rodham Clinton.

The author lives in Connecticut with her husband, Peter Karoczkai, and their three children.